Words That Walk Through Walls –

World Poets writing with İlhan Sami Çomak

Palewell Press

Words That Walk Through Walls –
World Poets writing with İlhan Sami Çomak

Edited by
Caroline Stockford
and Kelly Davis

Words That Walk Through Walls - World Poets writing
with İlhan Sami Çomak
First edition 2024 from Palewell Press,
www.palewellpress.co.uk
Printed and bound in the UK

ISBN 978-1-911587-93-4

İlhan's responses to John Macker, Blas Falconer, Menna
Elfyn, Alice Oswald, Jeffrey Cyphers Wright, Lee Herrick
and John Casquarelli previously appeared in *Separated from
the Sun* (2022). They are republished here by kind permission
of Smokestack Books.

A CIP catalogue record for this title is available from the
British Library.

Contents

Foreword

What you are about to read is a remarkable dialogue between Turkey's longest-serving student prisoner and some of the finest poets in Europe, New Zealand and the United States. This is a book of poems *for* and *with* İlhan Sami Çomak, who is still detained at the time of writing.

İlhan, who was studying geography at Istanbul University, was arrested in Turkey in 1994, when many Kurdish students and activists were arbitrarily detained. After 19 days of persistent torture he confessed to having lit a fire above Istanbul in the name of the separatist PKK (Kurdistan Workers' Party). He was found not guilty of this fabricated crime but was found to have engaged in separatist activities on behalf of the outlawed PKK. For this he was sentenced to life in prison, a total of 36 years. At the time of writing, İlhan has been in prison for 30 years.

During his incarceration, İlhan has had nine collections published, mostly lyrical nature poetry drawing on his childhood memories of growing up in a mountain village above Karlıova, near the south-eastern city of Bingöl, Turkey. In 2007 he won the Sennur Sezer Prize for Poetry and in 2021 the Metin Altıok Prize. Altıok, who taught at the school İlhan attended as a child, was assassinated, along with other Alevi literary figures and intellectuals, in a horrific arson attack on a hotel in Sivas in 1993.[1] On winning the Altıok Poetry Prize, İlhan said, 'It felt as though my teacher were still alive and had reached out his hand to pat my head, saying "Well done, İlhan!"' In addition to his

---

[1] 'an act of mob arson taking place on July 2, 1993 at the Hotel Madımak (Otel Madımak) in Sivas, Turkey, which resulted in the killing of 37 people, mostly Alevi intellectuals. Two perpetrators also died during the incident. The victims, who had gathered in the hotel for the Pir Sultan Abdal festival, were killed when a mob set fire to the hotel' – https://en.wikipedia.org/wiki/Sivas_massacre

poetry, he has written a best-selling autobiography[2] and a prize-winning play[3] about his life in prison.

Since 2001, İlhan has been visited regularly by a legal academic, Ms Ipek Özel. Ipek is İlhan's McKenzie Friend, a role that allows her to visit him weekly and to represent him with Power of Attorney in the outside world. Without Ipek, communication with İlhan – to the extent that has enabled the incredible exchanges in this book to take place – would have been impossible.

İlhan was denied his expected release on 20 August 2024, despite fulfilling the necessary term to qualify for parole. The prison parole board claimed that he had shouted political slogans four times and made unnecessary noise five times over a period of 30 years. His case for release will now be reconsidered every three months.

In 2020 PEN Norway[4] began to campaign for İlhan. This began with the translation of his first selected works in English, published by Smokestack Books in 2021 as *Separated from the Sun*. PEN Norway is grateful to the eight translators who worked on these poems. PEN Norway publicised İlhan's case and began to write to him and share his poetry. İlhan is now an honorary member of several PEN centres, spanning the world: Norway, Wales, Ireland, Austria, Sydney and San Miguel, Mexico. In 2021 İlhan won the Norwegian Authors Union Freedom of Expression Prize and in 2024 his poetry was published in Norwegian by Gyldendal. In 2022 an excerpt from

---

[2] 'How not to disturb the ants' nest', İletişim Publishing, İstanbul, 2021 https://iletisim.com.tr/kitap/karinca-yuvasini-dagitmamak/10033

[3] 'Life, I love you so' played to sold-out audiences in Istanbul and won 'Script of the Year' in the 2023 'Union of Theatre Critics' Awards'. The script was published as a book by İletişim Publishing: https://iletisim.com.tr/kitap/hayat-seni-cok-seviyorum/10248

[4] PEN Norway is an independent and non-profit membership organisation (part of the PEN International family of centres), dedicated to defending freedom of expression and supporting writers at risk and writers in prison. Oslo-based PEN Norway's goal is that everyone should have the right to express themselves freely. www.norskpen.no

Ilhan's poem 'What I Know of the Sea' was displayed on the London Underground Elizabeth Line trains as part of Poems on the Underground.

The Turkish poet Erkut Tokman was instrumental in producing this book. He had the idea that I, as PEN Norway's Turkey Adviser, should write poems with İlhan in a 'call and response manner'. These poems are included here, in translation from their original Turkish. Having embarked on this poetic collaboration, I then decided to reach out to world poets, asking them to write for İlhan.

The British-Hungarian poet George Szirtes contacted many poets in England, and the New York School poet John Casquarelli, now an academic at Koç University in Istanbul, did the same with American poets. The result was, quite simply, astonishing. Scores of American poets, many of them laureates and famous names, such as the Beat poet Anne Waldman, wrote to İlhan. The former Oxford Professor of Poetry Alice Oswald wrote the incredible 'Trial of the Soul by Physics', Ruth Padel wrote 'Pure Bright Experiment of Rain', and George Szirtes himself wrote for İlhan, and so too did many brilliant Irish poets, such as Theo Dorgan, Celia de Fréine and Leeanne Quinn. Menna Elfyn, President of Wales PEN Cymru, took the action further and has composed a poem a month for İlhan. His response to her poem 'The Piper' is one of the most touching in the book, with its opening lines:

> I give praise to the embraces of women
> that reach right into my cell...

İlhan replied to many poems he received from world poets with poems of his own.

The process of making these words 'walk through walls' was a long one. First the poems were translated from English to Turkish; and then came their workshopping by a group of dedicated translators, before they were sent to Ipek Özel, İlhan's visitor. Ipek would print them out and take them weekly to the prison to hand over to the management. She would leave home at 5am to reach the prison by 7am. Once every four weeks, she could meet İlhan face to face. She would tell him of the events taking place for him in the outside world and of the PEN centres, poets and long-standing supporters' actions for him. Ipek would receive İlhan's poems written back to the world in hand-written form, on official, stamped prison paper.

PEN Norway is immensely grateful to all the translators who worked on the project, some of whom do not wish to be named, to George Szirtes, John Casquarelli and to all the PEN centres who have made İlhan their honorary member and who have held events for him. Irish PEN have featured İlhan twice in book fairs, and another event is planned for the Dublin Book Festival in November 2024, just before İlhan is due to be considered for parole once more.

International solidarity means far more to the imprisoned writer than most of us imagine. PEN Congresses have heard from poets such as Enoh Myomesse of Cameroon,[5] who said that when he started receiving sackfuls of letters from PEN members around the world, 'The prison guards began to treat me much better, and to call me a VIP, a Very Important Prisoner.' At PEN's 90th International Congress in Oxford in September 2024, Kurdish journalist Nedim Türfent[6] said, of his detention for writing a newspaper article in 2016, 'At first those who arrested me were discussing whether or not to kill me. The guards began to show me Tweets about me from PEN International and English PEN, protesting my detention, and I think this changed their mind.'

In a letter İlhan wrote in January 2020 (published on the 'free the poet' website) he said, of international solidarity:

The fact that my writings reach you and that you make my voice heard enables me to heal as it allows me the satisfaction

---

[5] https://www.theguardian.com/books/2015/apr/29/enoh-meyomesse-cameroon-poet-activist-released-from-prison-freedom-of-speech

[6] https://www.englishpen.org/pen-writes/penwrites-nedim-turfent/

of explaining what happened to me and how I feel. In this way I heal and grow in strength. Malice cannot impede the imagination! My poetry must be proof of this.

[…]

If you can have one at hand, please read a stanza or a poem of mine and share it with others. […] By reading my poems you will have looked warmly into my eyes, also. My heart is comforted by your solidarity efforts. Do not give up on your prayers, please. In the hope that we will meet in freedom!

With love, İlhan Sami Çomak[7]

Special thanks go to the publisher of this book, Camilla Reeve of Palewell Press, who along with its co-editor Kelly Davis, was at one of the first solidarity meetings for İlhan in London at the Poetry Café in February 2020, hosted by Exiled Writers Ink.[8] Both have been great supporters of İlhan and have worked unstintingly to bring these beautiful poems to readers.

İlhan belongs back in the world, in a world he still dearly loves and longs for, as attested by his own lines. We say free the poet! Return İlhan to the world so that we may all hear from him, hear him perform, hear what he has to say and meet him in person.

Caroline Stockford, PEN Norway, October 2024

---

[7] https://ilhancomak.wordpress.com/2020/07/24/letter-from-ilhan-january-2020/

[8] https://www.exiledwriters.co.uk/2020-2/

Publisher's Preface

This is a very special anthology, full of shared humanity and admiration for İlhan Sami Çomak as a poet and a person, but also resonating with world poets' grieving anger at his prolonged imprisonment. Among many wonderful poems, these lines by Theo Dorgan, at the start of Section 3, echo my concern for İlhan's situation: 'From some deep chamber of the heart / I mount a blessing on my breath and / bounce it off the moon.'

We received so many poems that the book grew from an idea in Caroline Stockford's mind to an unwieldy manuscript. This necessitated omitting some submissions, shortening some biographies, and leaving poems written by Turkish and Kurdish poets to appear in the Turkish-language anthology due to be published in Istanbul. But we want to thank all those who offered their poems. Your support for İlhan, as for all prisoners of conscience, is vital for his mental and physical wellbeing.

Many people helped to bring the book into being. We are particularly indebted to Caroline Stockford, John Casquarelli, George Szirtes and Erkut Tokman for reaching out to poets and translators, and managing their submissions and translations.

Because this is such an international anthology, we chose to keep both UK-English and US-English spellings unchanged as received from each English-language poet. And we tried to faithfully incorporate Turkish and other languages' accents. As publisher, I apologise for any failure to achieve that aim.

Sincere thanks must go to all the translators. Where a poem is not in its original language, the translator's name follows the author's name below the poem. However, we also want to acknowledge those who translated English-language poems into Turkish so İlhan could read them; and Ipek Özel for taking poems into the prison and bringing us his responses.

As publisher, I am deeply grateful to Kelly Davis for her patient, dedicated editing and her advice. It takes a community to create a book. I'm honoured that Palewell Press belongs to that community.

Camilla Reeve, Palewell Press

POEMS TO İLHAN
AND HIS RESPONSES

*İlhan's poems were translated
into English by Caroline Stockford.
The Norwegian poets translated their own poems.*

Exile

If I stay out here in this spring garden
exile long enough, the sun will return.
They say at the bottom of the gravest doubt
there is satori: I'm
missing their life stories already
their voices compatible with all the other voices
the cordiality, timorousness or bravery
of their unfinished sentences.

I follow a shovel into the earth. This is what
the *desert* once was, a brazen hike through
unaccounted for territory, where the
prayers, always works in progress,
rose like smoke signals
easily believed and dispersed.

No answers
from the government or the bobble-headed Poe
figure all dressed in black on my desk or the
photo on my wall of the firing line of Apaches
    fighting terrorism since 1492.

To reconcile what matters most with what might not
these brazen sorrows
                        first apricot tree blossoms
puncture the warming air.

John Macker

İlhan's response to John Macker

You rightly say I've stayed so long in exile
in this well, the sun never returning!
I still have a yearning within me for light.
I love the sun, and the loop of the moon
I see so little of. Each spring the steam
flies up from warming soil. I'm as far from spring,
soil and steam as a severed hand.

Still I piece all that I miss into a single picture.
Into that wounded bird called freedom.
I must do it, so I won't forget.
Life is severe, defiant and all walled
because I'm here. I say: the blossoms
of the first cherry tree, breaking into air,
How do they smell? Can you tell me this
and what their colour is?
I seem to have forgotten.

For a Spell

You dip the end of the small plastic wand
into the soapy water, hold it
to your mouth, and blow gently, so
the iridescent film
within the serrated ring
trembles as it grows and grows, until
you are—*we are*—in it,
all that *has ever* or *will ever* waits
outside the bubble, which floats, now,
slowly to the ground.

*

When a bubble floats to the ground
it means something is about

to break. A spell can be
broken. We say, *You fall*

under a spell the way
we say *you fall*

in love. *For a spell* means, an undefined,
but short period of time,

as in, *For a spell, we didn't want
anything else.*

Blas Falconer

İlhan's response to Blas Falconer

I have a need for levity
for balloons that quiver and expand, that take
from me the heavy burden of life; of time.
Like the line of the register, I need lightness
like the resilience of fruit pips,
the silent passing that reaps all seasons,
strength of labourers' calloused hands,
the distance at which men and women
walk together, protecting the fresh,
new feelings of beginnings.

I need the unquestionable survival of trees,
The will of starlings to shoal the sky
and the lightness this lends me.
When my journey is heavier than heavy,
stretching longer and longer,
I tell myself to believe in magic,
even if it's short or fleeting.

Like, when clouds trail up and off,
I stare at their feet and that joy of blue
until my whole self takes the side of beauty.
And ask, should I favour being filled
with love's radiant pomegranate?
Say what you will, I'm ready to believe.

Star Harbor

*...labour to keep alive in your breast
that little celestial fire called conscience.
—George Washington*

If only for tonight, follow me past the last
lilac that's blooming in flames of silence.
Here, on the final block before the river,
the east wind comes seeking solace.
We moan in chorus. The tea kettle joins in.

Tonight, I trip on blue stairs chasing Orion,
hunting for game in the cosmos.
The game lives inside us. The window
never worries about becoming a widow.
Tonight, my candle channels your vision.

Jeffrey Cyphers Wright

İlhan's response to Jeffrey Cyphers Wright

Before looking to that clean corner of shade and budding lilac
I washed my face and hands with copious water.

Now, so refreshed. Resolute as a drop
on the rim of a glass, in its will to find ground.

Taken in by your words I passed a time or two,
following you: How good that I did.

In case there is no rock, let the East Wind take refuge in
    my body.
May it shelter in the ringing of our voices as we sing songs
    by moonlight.

And don't forget, please don't forget: the outstretched hand of
the river accompanies us too. In meadow's taste is
    knowledge of far distant places.

I saved myself from stumbling before, and will, once more,
And yet 'the weight of the world is love'*, is love, is love...

My fears are all within me, my freedom too.
Barren minds weigh down dark night
and the devotion of moonlight.

Light one more candle, please.
A candle to accompany 'the weight of the world'.*

Let us protect the trembling flame.

*From 'Song' by Allen Ginsberg

The Trial of the Soul by Physics

Tired I am tired of the rules
I am so tired of the same old
      limitless justice of the light
and the trial of the soul by physics

who can I shout at if I shout
it is the same strict softness
    as lifts the leaves
that breezily descends and snuffs it out

how come the dew by means of evaporation
and certain seeds
    by means of tiny hairs and fans
get away on a wisp of air

what's missing what should have been thought of here
   is a thousand foot folded sheet of gold
stepped and tapering into space
like a tilted beam of God

or at least a ladder
leaning into these rain-worn trees
with two steel rails and its feet refracted in the river

so that slowly the soul with trailing watersleeves
and silted shoes could get out
and then another and another

the way mosquitos stand around in groups on the water
fixing their broken struts and all
   suddenly crookedly ascend

Alice Oswald

İlhan's response to Alice Oswald

And I'd hidden in my dreams the cooing doves.
I sought the tired trees and your hands
in my body's harmony with another.
Hid unguarded smiles of flowers from the wrath of the wind.

In the beginning, I said it was endless. The crucifix of the desert
entered time's eyes, slipped, knowing the ruggedness of earth,
slipped, breaking the mirror of existence and nothing.
Fright took form in my body, came and sat in life's voice.
Were I to scream, my mouth would but summon the void!

For there is a weight that holds the soul to objects,
grace that carries seeds to far-off places.
The fresh white of a cloud, desire inclining us to flight.
The lightness of scentless rain and snow and more, and more.
Things that give soul to our souls.

We're one, with all objects, just so!

When My Journey Becomes a Pirouette

Do you take the time to listen
      to each drop of a leaking faucet?
Like tears that contain a multitude
      of memories and doubts.
Maybe the drain is a wormhole
      leading to a galaxy of velvet, silk,
and cheap cologne, two buttons
      opened on a short-sleeved denim
shirt that hides growls of thunder
      in my chest and a torrential downpour
in the stomach. Hunger belongs to
      all seasons. Let us eat what the forest
provides, drink from the running brook.
      The dragonfly is the poet's metaphor,
the paintbrush's stroke on the
      morning canvas. How I long to fly,
yet learn from Icarus' lesson.
      When next the stars weep, I will
greet them with wings extended.

John Casquarelli

İlhan's response to John Casquarelli

I place my notebook before me,
and life expands exponentially!
But I long for the forests: geometry of green.
Want the other side of light and dark;
other side of the cool of morning.
Sometimes I think of the stream,
bathing in waters I thought were all mine,
in childlike excitement,

Opening my arms in those wingless days
pretending to be a bird! Immeasurable heat
of the sun mixed with plenteous thunder of rain.
I stop and listen to the dripping tap, listen
to seedlings as they pierce earth. Yes, I listen
to the tedious onrush of time with tears
for my memories! All that's denied to me
calls to earth and in the name of longing.

Laughing and crying I stretch a hand, for ever,
to all colours, fragile as a stemless rose.
Yes, hunger is a beast of all seasons.
But love is everywhere!

The Piper

See the gentle bird there, by your window,
startled by you, so pensive in your cell,
spare some crumbs to this little fellow
to mark his arrival as he wishes you well.
Listen to the melody, what a gift
a poet's accent, its harmony restarts
another song, an aria to uplift
and beat in the sweet poet's tender heart.

And perhaps he'll fly away, message
    deliverer
to the land of your boyhood, bright message ablaze;
share with other mountain birds. Piper in gorse
    and heather –
a message of longing, *hiraeth* as he sings your praise.
His wings will reverberate of your captivity,
folk song of hope for the blue sky of liberty.

Menna Elfyn

I have acknowledged a famous Welsh language poet
T.E. Nicholas (1879–1971) who was imprisoned during
the Second World War on false charges. He was a pacifist
and held Communist ideals. He wrote 150 poems in prison
which were smuggled out. Written on prison toilet paper,
they were published in 1942 to great acclaim.
He wrote one poem to a bird near his cell
which I have reimagined here.

*Hiraeth – a kind of homesickness that can also
mean a longing, nostalgia and yearning for a home that
you cannot return to, that no longer exists, or maybe never was.*

İlhan's response to Menna Elfyn

I give praise to the embraces of women
that reach right into my cell.
I give praise to the wind's own knowing
that it is wind. I am without a door, yet my wings
splay wide as an atlas. Birds love me.
I hear that delight in their songs
and the quiet of these blues and greens
gives me peace. There is a stairway
that leads to the very height of life.

I love the birds because we're brothers in hunger,
as the window creaks with tiredness in its frame.
So then sing your song, beautiful bird.
Let us go blazing to the seas, to my childhood,
when I believed in all the stories, to the times when
I fell and fell, grazing my knees,
to the pain of my hand when it would bleed.
To the wound of the skies and the earth.
To the pure, bright experiment of rain.
I am with the birds.
Life accepts me again.

In a Daydream

Say there is a field.

In it, a horse. You have not seen
one in over fifteen years, I read.
It is indigenous to your country
much like your dreaming:
a wilderness no state can own,
where the horse, like the dream,
can take flight and land
on a cloud. İlhan, here is a true
story, separate from the horse
or the daydream. I was born
in South Korea and adopted
to the United States. I was
ten months old. I don't know
if I was lost, abandoned, given,
or stolen, but now I write
poems and know they kept me
alive. What a blessing
to place words near each other
to help us breathe. Someday
I hope we can share a walk
in a field and see a horse.
You would know more
about them than I ever would,
I believe. How they see.
How they run. How their calm
grace keeps us in light.

Lee Herrick

İlhan's response to Lee Herrick

We had a celebrated pasture, that stroked
my child's head with tenderness. We called it
'Tapë Kozikan' in Kurdish: Peak of Trenches.
It took its name with Russian occupation, pre-WWI.
I saw no trenches, just empty, bleached-out cartridges.
I took its name to heart, like an old memory.

On Tapë Kozikan I rode my first horse. A chestnut.
Accepting me, thanks to its biddable breeding.
Bareback, I gripped its mane, its bright skin swarmed
my legs like a warm wave. The horse's power made itself
    known,
and I suffused the Spring with laughter.

His name was Koçe, he smelled clean, like someone
from the same house. I had no fear. Do we learn it
    retrospectively?
So I say: The horses that sweat and gallop in my poems
all assume the shape of Koçe.

Your poem filled the void of my lost past with a fresh breath.
Poetry is on the side of the weak, a nameless bud,
giving height to those who wish to fly. One day,
let's walk at Tapë Kozikan with the joy of children
playing hide-and-seek. Let's walk, walk, walk,
until we smell the lofty scent of a horse.

You ride on the horse with your tiredness
and your words, and I will hold the halter.
Friendship like that is such a thing!

Limitless

I stretch my arms above my head
I try to reach what I have lost
They call it limitless
No end, no beginning
They call it limitless

Øivind Hånes

İlhan's response to Øivind Hånes

No need to stretch your arms toward the limitless
you've already got infinity!
I want to talk to you about freedom,
smells rushing through lungs in turmoil,
and poetry with the pretty names
of the winds we know and do not know
that bring old rivers to life.
In the beginning was poetry! Let us have faith!
Not with the certainty of reason,
not with the pain of lost lives,
but with that grand possibility, constructed
and completed by poetry,
Let us have faith.

Not according to the Gospel of John do I say this:
In the beginning there was poetry!
And poetry became life! And just like that
everything came into being!
The voice of poetry is Infinity!

Letter to a Captive

the one from darkness locked in
is cultivating sun rays in the mind
the one who's been deprived of light
is the one who has dreamt it

Torgeir Rebolledo Pedersen

İlhan's response to Torgeir Rebolledo Pedersen

Darkness came up to my ankles
then up to my knees but never up to my mind!
Water is more fluid because thinking makes it so.
The sea is rough with all my longing.
So bright the sun shines! It's my sun
because I willed it so. Life is conceived
in my thoughts but always too late for me.
I like inexperience! I long for the warmth of
people and brotherhood –
because you only seek what you've lost.
I enjoy the finding and losing again
and the wonder of being able to create!

Some Lines to İlhan

When nature is my crown of feathers
If I gave you my small, sacred lies
Behind the birdsong is a song in a song from another song

I remember
Spring, spring, and summer,
summer

Aasne Linnestå

İlhan's response to Aasne Linnestå

I've been hit so many times
I don't remember anymore
the beauty of carrying an umbrella
while walking in the rain.
I'm on an eternal road. No poppies,
no winding rivers.
And I miss the smell of earth.
I want to be told off by my mother
because I muddied my trousers.
I don't know about spring, only winter.
I know the vicious cold penetrating my soul.
I accept your small sacred lies!
I accept the birdsong!
I accept the taste of figs, the juniper seed,
the crowded street. You reminded me
of spring. Spring and summer.
I thank you so much!

A River Can't Help but Run

Magma is hot. Sand shifts.
Volcanoes release. Peacocks deceive,
ladybugs too. The scorpion
is simply a scorpion. The shark is
simply a shark. A star is
a star but gone long before
we see it. When I like to feel
grounded but the ground starts to move.
Magma is fertile. Whales enjoy
the water. Humans are
the virus here.
The birds are confused,
saplings too.
The leaves brown
only to turn green again
too soon.

Gabriel Don

Ilhan's response to Gabriel Don

There are some things I must tell you
about the never-moving ratio of damp,
of pairing the name of god with grief,
of scorpions who seek their own sting,
the attitude of water and the capacity
of ladybirds for cannibalism...
My hair is getting wet in the rain: I'll tell you
of the traces we leave when we walk
whilst loving and blaming,
how I stretch to see the window
that will not let the sun go
as it lengthens to eternity,
I'll tell of the permanence of crucifix marks
on the hands and the feet, and the imprint
of vanity left by your saying –
'there exists a mountain, and I
will compete with the mystery of its peak!'
– this is what we call human, isn't it?

Let us not touch the way the stream knows illuminance.
If the mind seeds itself it's always a mistake.
Let us leave nature to flow unto itself.

Swimmer

There is warm weather today
He writes from prison says
he does not know Wordsworth
But that moving from reading
To writing is his necessity if
The spirit is to stay alive.

How does the spirit stay alive
When the flowers grow beyond
The bars and in the mountain
Villages snowdrops gather in
Clusters free and unashamed?

He does not think he deserves
The title 'poet' more a teller
Of tales a chronicler it's more
Important to be human open
Loosed from evil nothingness.

He is a swimmer who has to swim
Because he is in the sea
Because each wave threatens
Because wild currents will move
Him too quickly from the land.

Swimming is what one does
A moving body is rhythm
Hands arms and legs unite
Bright breath dreams its way
Eyes set on safe blue hills.

He writes daily from prison
Like the bravest of swimmers
He'll reach the fabled shore of love
But when when when even
As long seasons drift on teach
Discipline of things and surprise.

Michael Baron

Life does not lie

I am between moon and tide, between whisper and scream.
When I was a child, had still the script of child,
when I was hostage to my mother's pomegranate smile,
when I looked from the window to the full light of the garden,
watching the practical philosophy of hands plucking the
    fruit tree,
in those times, when we still heard the sounds of frogs,
when women passed through my life and the lake was blue,
I knew the value of blue.
I understand there is pain, too, on the steps of life.

On the day of existence, the wind rose up to meet me.
Resistance sat like dew on the grass, meeting my feet.
Ripe fires grew across my body and doves –
my feelings were met by the rustle of their wings.
In spring's demeanour I hear the sounds of cleaning,
the footsteps of plains and mountains, I hear the law
of snow, melting. Earth grows damp in my memory.

Fruit ripens. Stone's habitual weight grows light,
makes it flow and tremble as it wishes. In my place
between trouble and well-being I hear the song
of happiness from the world as good will blossoms.
'Life does not lie,' I say. 'It does not lie!'

From Geldim Sana

POEMS BY İLHAN AND CAROLINE STOCKFORD

In March 2020, İlhan Sami Çomak and Caroline Stockford sent each other five separate stanzas by post. They wrote in Turkish, and each responded to the other's opening stanza with one or more of their own. The poems were translated between Turkish and English by Caroline and Turkish poet and editor Erkut Tokman.

Time in the Ripening of Fruit

I had a pomegranate, quinces, I spent time in
the ripening of fruit. It was morning. And they
saw the summer sun overflow from me.
With the eternal beauty of my childhood
I said, *Fall down, you mountain! Cease, you winds!*
They threw stones at me. We got there, and they
threw stones at me. I was sleepless. The birds
were warbling in full flow. The waters were torpid,
my steps a little rushed. I said, *The names of flowers*
are spinning in my head, their memories, their scents
are trembling on and on. But they threw stones at me
from that place called life.
Did you see? Did anyone?

I won't turn my head away, and there's no escape
from now. We are what it means to live, it's us.
And all the stones we touch will one day return
to sand. The hand of patience puts everything
in its place, in time. I can't tell this to the weary
mountains, or the fretful seas, they are both
older than me. Birds fly over heads of
good and bad, led on by vibrations.
And if it reflects our face, does water
not also see us? We wear the things we know
like new brooches. The mountains are laughing
at us, showers of falling stones chuckling.
In my hand I will catch every stone they threw at you.

Stanza 1: İlhan Sami Çomak, Silivri Prison
Stanza 2: Caroline Stockford, Bristol

Miracles Delivered on the Wind

How much of flight is wind, how much the bird?
How much the stubborn call of freedom?
Branches follow the logic of light
and the natural miracle of reaching.
We must reach out. What do leaves think,
occupied with the green business of living?
They feel the tug of nature's simple bridle
and read libraries of weeds. Let us walk
nder the oak trees. Let us, too, read their poetry.

There's something the wind knows!
As it opens an ornate page for the bird
in the commanding shadow of its wing.
Page made from the dizzy branch of flying skywards,
from blue's most silent days. A page,
wide, quick-witted, a little capricious,
yet simple, with the stillness of a lake-side.
This is what we called freedom!
The stubborn stars have their gaze fixed on existence.
But let us talk instead of the look of leaves
on the trunk stretched up and on by the patronage of roots.
Let us talk of the abstract and envious volume of time.
I am preoccupied with living. My waiting,
brimming with thirst, is on the side of the birds.
It favours the miracles delivered on the wind.
Look into the pupils of existence!
My poetry is of light and leaves.
My poetry favours hearing the footsteps of freedom.

Stanza 1: Caroline Stockford, Bristol
Stanza 2: İlhan Sami Çomak, Silivri Prison

Incidence of Joy

I entered your words like a story book
and got lost in the forest of meaning.
I found the clearing steeped in sunshine
and there I saw your words in a spring pool.
They swim like white fish, light particles
stretching to transparency. I swam in your poems
and was renewed. To be with all and one
is an instant revolution, bloodless, painless,
a timeless transformation. You are so too,
and so is poetry. Space is between us, and art.
In the endless meadows I feel constrained
There's a whole world in you, your view, four walls.
Is not the great world a cage, for the closed-minded?

I am purified by memories.
With the kernel from the fruit I stole in childhood
I will knock down all the walls.
Peaches, plums and nectarines, many a cherry.
The original revolution began with love,
with knowing the first wet taste of pears in my mouth.
With the tenderness of how I miss my mother
touching my forehead, my hair –
My words have come out of the sun!
Like a horse; a horse that parts the tide of crowds,
like the wind, swaying drunk behind a kite,
and the unpassing sorrow of my sock when it steps in water.

I multiply it, multiply and renew time.
I write my self.
The doveless days of no garden,
the loops of season I can feel, the solitudes that kiss fear.
It is hopeless for you to say, 'I love you'
Your saying so is just an incidence of joy,
solid patience of embracing with desire –
That which overflows belongs to all!
My window looks out at a wall!

Stanza 1: Caroline Stockford, Bristol
Stanza 2: İlhan Sami Çomak, Silivri Prison

We are Beholden to Water

Waves on the beach attain their smoothest state.
I feel the pulse of their splashing as it rushes to silence.
The wave that hits the beach smooths the path of its return.
Let no one sense the magic of this turning point!
Islands are but old mountain peaks; no separation
in the deep. Mountains hold hands underwater
and feel no envy of the greatness of others.
We are one planet when viewed from ocean's floor.
Are we not one in the realms that we can't see?

They say that waves, wishing to awake, sought the voice
    of wind.
All things return, return; are held in their own embrace.
In the abiding law of water and creation.
So, the wave that hits the shore smooths the path of its return.
And the echo is whetted by colliding with solitude.
Let us snap awake with the cracking of a branch
for we are beholden to water, as are the trees.
We know how to see, and so do the birds.
We wash in the river, as fishes bathe in consciousness of water.
We love our little ones, as do the cats
and our love is no higher than theirs.
It's a lie that mountains covets mountains! Our lie.
Sky and earth belong to no-one.
We are here. With goodness we should live.
With goodness and a levelling of all roads.

Stanza 1: Caroline Stockford, Bristol
Stanza 2: İlhan Sami Çomak, Silivri Prison

Rain Dream

Spring comes like a rain dream.
I awaited its coming, all at once I was soaked.
Everything was water, suddenly, everything green
and the beginning had long since begun.
For those who know it well, each day is spring,
each day is spring for those made out of poetry.
The youthfulness of May festooned on the trees
falls upon us like grains of pollen.
We become one with it, with our breathing.
We are spring, we are May, we are eternal.
Are you with us this spring?

With rain's dream and scent of flowers
you invite me to the arms of May.
I think of distant times; seasons like childhood,
like youth. My feet trip with the tone of eternity.
I'll come, of course! I know the very spring of Spring!
May brings me such thrilling gifts; the word's adolescence,
radiance of single letters. And poetry takes me by the hand.
I know the bright beginning, and how to amass darkness.
I touch all the world's beauties with the sun's own fingertips;
know well how to relish the pleasure of touch.
I will come to Spring. Wait for me!
Let's open May's gate as one, that rain may
make our dreams multiply.
I know the very spring of Spring!

Stanza 1: Caroline Stockford, Bristol
Stanza 2: İlhan Sami Çomak, Silivri Prison

The Mind's Fresh Rose

Not our hands but our minds reach out to you.
Our thoughts seek you like migrating birds.
A search party set out. They drank your words
like spring water. Where will they find you?

I told them: look in poetry's core!
Filiality is a wave that touches the sand,
its difference felt even when it has returned.
Hand in hand they arrive, the small waves,
going as far as they can go.

They gather together, those who don't know
each other, those who love you, and in the
venn diagram we conceive – is you, is poetry.
Come, at last, come!

Sometimes I meet with the softness of migrating birds,
with the care with which my friends touch flowers,
those friends who embrace me with their senses.
And where will they find me?

Watch the clouds, please! Draw in, as much as you can,
the scent of earth. See how the cats weave with each other
    saucily.
See the shining colour of weeds at the foot of the fence?
And where will they find me?

Deserts have their tranced philosophy, but let us love the rain!
Sky is plain and blue but let us love the dirt of earth!
Darkness has beauty, and is necessary, but let us love
    ascendancy of light!
Chains may bear circles, but let us love the androgyny of law!

They may find me in my sayings, this and that, in other things,
Friends are the mind's fresh rose, the white rose, red rose,
unfading and reaching out to me.
I lighten.

And where will they find me? In poetry.
In those things within, and left out of my poetry.
In human warmth, which is everlasting.

Stanzas 1, 2, 3: Caroline Stockford, Bristol
Stanzas 4, 5, 6, 7, 8: İlhan Sami Çomak, Silivri Prison

Towards the Day

I remain like a glass sphere in all this chaos.
Not the slightest movement.
I sewed a robe from the sky
dark as diamond, bright as coal
and opened the door to my self.
In the corporeal castle's dungeon
is a tunnel to the light.
The well inside me: a tower.
To scale it, my struggle.
Why do I memorise so many stories?
Telling is the contract of knowing.
Where does it lead – the path inside you?

Time is everywhere!
I try to understand how activity of bodies
and disembodiment can fold themselves
into existence with a weary will.
I used to be there in the skies! Setting out
on my paths to learn eternity by rote
and I was so well, then. Close to flight,
the Tree of Life lent me a branch
before evil learned me inch by inch, by heart.
I wanted to believe in reason.
But it became an axe, evil personified as
human, it memorised my every part.

I remain like a glass sphere, yes, a little
motionless. But there is always light!
A tunnel, and new paths
waiting to be trodden. I hear
that pleasant voice, of reality,
as visions crack open the doors,
lifting me up from ash, from the well,
towards the day.

I suit well the skies!

**Stanza 1: Caroline Stockford, Bristol
Stanza 2: İlhan Sami Çomak, Silivri Prison**

Shine Without Shadow

Perhaps they tell you my name,
as my face breaks up in a broken mirror.
What do you expect from a silhouette?
Let water pour from my tear-filled eyes
and let us go silent together,
time and again, in darkness.
So that different scents may mature,
rising from the body of life, flowing to us,
around us. Filling to fullness, with all-new aromas.
Other suns are dawning, can you see them?
At last the knot of love is being undone.
I've been embraced, I've seen, I've come.

If we have no names how can we be known?
Your inner sea is clear in poetry.
I don't know the face of the new-born moon.
Let the knot of love unfold like a flower.
Let it shine without shadow, as soft
as April's suns. I can't see the new star,
its shining power is blinding.
I open my eyes in the cinnamon garden.
At last, courage is blooming like spring buds.
My burden lends its weight to earth,
my back is light, oh life! I am embraced.

Stanza 1: İlhan Sami Çomak, Silivri Prison
Stanza 2: Caroline Stockford, Bristol

Swimming like a Yellow Ghost

First I thought of the freshness of the shade
in which I hide. The sound of the city,
mountain's distant grandeur. And the clumsy
attempts of fledglings as they try to land
on branches. I grew thirsty, so thirsty, and
thought of other lives. I thought long and
hard, with no view on which to rest my eyes,
of darkness and the sun. My mind asks,
What is it to thrust out green leaves?
What is it to work, build up a sweat,
to tire thanks to labour, from beautiful
hard work? No matter in which stream
I bathe, the waters are so bitter.

Look! See your form in the shaded corner
of the lake. There floats the crown of a daffodil
swimming like a yellow ghost. Its petals
are seeping towards the silence of transparency.
There is strength in the ellipses, where petals
overlap, we are strong in the space we make
between us. Come, let us climb Idris's high
mountain, let the brave memories of your
muscles return. Let sweat shine, and not tears.

Stanza 1: İlhan Sami Çomak, Silivri Prison
Stanza 2: Caroline Stockford, Bristol

At a Quarter to Dawn

Let me tell you of waters today,
of the smell of cut roses in baskets,
of my desire to climb the willow tree
and of longings that have faded to memories.
To tell you how the anger is sown, when
my mind plays its broken record, calling
Life tripped me up! It went and tripped me up!
Where will the sun rise? I want to talk
about this and the most simple reasons for crying
in the rain. The sky has a strange way of caressing.
There is a sound to budding leaves and to
forgottenness. The sun will be born from my palm!
I want to tell you about this, and of the trembling
of the wind that swims over my body.

Your body is a tree, each leaf is a poem,
the curious wind plays every one, and we,
on our far islands, hear the music of your news.
We measure endings with the setting sun.
Ceaseless star that will not stop, pouring gold.
Tell me the rain's secrets, on the mountain
slopes at a quarter to dawn. I would tell you,
too, of the vision of that day, when I saw the
horizon rise up, of the inner worlds of patience
and possibility, but you know all these better
than me. Tell me of your miracles, I'm listening.

Stanza 1: İlhan Sami Çomak, Silivri Prison
Stanza 2: Caroline Stockford, Bristol

Bell of a First Kiss

Light hits the seas within me.
The questions are immense.
Like freshness rising from fine climates,
like I'm gathering flowers, gathering
countless pleasures from touch.
Breeze is blowing from the future.
My breath corrals the excitement.
Remind me of the law of the wave,
fluent and formidable.
Let life become new! Let hunger rise up
from just-made bread, and
the thought of poppies wet
by new rain grow clearer.
Your lip is red with the taste of a first kiss,
bring new fires with your body,
I'll wash myself anew.

The sea's law is made by its wave, it turns
back to wildness the green glass surface,
waves run far from origin, to abate
on the sand, they return, depleted.
We call to one another from our white
wooden boats, I look for you each time I
crest a ridge. You are there, and children
write your poems on the beach.
The bell of a first kiss is on my tongue, I
have forgotten everyone.
I've grown deaf in this world of war cries.
I need the sea and your dazzling.
With poems we fling a lasso at sky.
Suddenly I'm flying.
Yes, life becomes new.

**Stanza 1: İlhan Sami Çomak, Silivri Prison
Stanza 2: Caroline Stockford, Bristol**

OTHER POEMS
FOR İLHAN

Lone Voyager

The boat pulls on through the night,
steady and sure. I lash the helm
and go below, light up the GPS.
On Google Earth I have found
the exact co-ordinates of the prison,
the exact distance from this point
on the rolling bosom of the water.
I move the cursor and mark the bearing.
On deck again with a handheld compass
I orient myself as the foresail cracks and fills.

From some deep chamber of the heart
I mount a blessing on my breath and
bounce it off the moon – it curves off
and down to where, on a bare patch
of parched blue-lit concrete, a yard
deep inside high white walls, a flower
stands modest in the still air. I call
from the drifting mist of silence three drops
of dew to fall delicate on the yellow petals,
to slide with infinite grace to the very root.

Theo Dorgan

Hum

11 December 2020

I am writing this
with the light of a torch
on the face of the sea.
I am writing the sea
in the heart of a conch,
the whispers of shells
in the whorls of the ear,
in the ear of the world
held low to the ground,
to the hum of the rails,
the vibration of bars.
The tremors of iron
that steal down the spine,
the spine of the guard
who is closing his ears
to the flute of the bird
that turns in its cage,
to the pencil's scratch
on the field of the page.

Isobel Dixon

For İlhan

Each day, walking beside the sea,
I think of what it means to be unfree.

A winter sea can terrorise the shore
And put at risk the trawlerman and sailor.

Their choice is stark: they must be brave
Until the sea settles again, wave on wave.

In a Turkish prison, you are braver still,
Long years have failed to break your will.

Inside you, a secret place survives:
The cosmos where your poetry thrives.

Liz McManus, PEN na hÉireann

Dream of the Tree

The dream of the tree looks the same
at the beginning as it will at the end.
Insects burrow the dark, dream
in the soil. The dream reaches the roots
of the tree that is not burning.
The tree is not dreaming in the way
the insects dream, or the other animals
that are dreaming in the forest.
Shelter is not the same as hiding,
fire not the same as burning.
The tree's dream can often be disturbed
by an axe, or a knife
carving a human name.
The tree notes the knife
as it notes the insect bite
at the edge of a leaf.
But the tree cannot be
expelled from its dream
the way people are.
The dream of the tree
is a dream of any season,
of any forest, of any flame.

Leeanne Quinn

Birds Give All They Know to Their Wings

Open the door to the retina,
the brain infuses to a single
      3 dimensional image
Physiological imagination, we need you
Light through the chinks of mind
We need your tactile imagination
Open the door to the phenomenal world
The writing on this page, miles away
I feel your compassion as it flies

Lands on stem of leaves and flowers
Of one pointed mind.
The wilting lily, o lily of my childhood
In a city of speed and forbidden impulse
Lily at the window, welcome her wellbeing
Rooted in a lotus-symbol, born of mud
Welcome the multitudes I know you are there
For one another and the lone poet who can sing
Of human perception
Freedom for heart, hand, justice
Who sings of dancing with existence

Earlier the flicker, a bird of toil
Rare in a city yard
Boring his holes in the trunk of a soft tree
The world at risk in its ignorance of love & sound
& innocence, but is welcomed as utopia
In narrations of hermetic worlds bursting to be heard
And the bird giving all it knows, no manipulation

Open the door, ear & eye

Anne Waldman

Waiting Time, Autumn

We don't see the prisoner, not in any season.
The prisoner is invisible like the soul.
The prisoner *is* the soul and as long as the prisoner exists
no one is free.
As long as the prisoner exists the soul is only pieces
without a root without a home without a human being.
And still I am free and fortunate,
still I have all visible beauty
like the autumn flowers and the glowing leaves.

The garden is full of perennials that rot and smell sweet
and the berries of the rowan trees light up the grove.
Under the reading lamp at night
the rivers overflow the map
and the poem you wrote in your cell is becoming
a more open house in my house
You, in your cell, is the autumn's clear thought
or a life lived as *one* thought, *one* longing, *one* vision.

Steinar Opstad
Line in italics is by İlhan Sami Çomak

Rowan

If I could, I'd send you a *llatai*
in your captivity.
A key is not permitted.
I can't send the air of my country
or a jar of rain that makes
my country infamous.

I send you a leaf
from a rowan tree –
beautiful for you to hold
in both hands.
In its veins a secret message
Criafolen, criaf -o- len.
A cry behind a veil.
And a song's murmur
as you walk one day
towards her and gaze
from her branches
at the sky's unveiling gift of *awen*.

Menna Elfyn

*Llatai – an old Welsh poetic device that accompanied
a gift (of a horse, dove, or any object).
Criafolen – mountain ash or rowan tree.
Awen – inspiration (particularly poetic inspiration)
or flowing energy.*

Words

It was a chance encounter – I was taking
my usual walk, he was visiting for the day.
The hills could be seen in the distance,
linking sides all the way up the coast.

We stood there for about fifteen minutes,
deep in conversation, both of us knowing
our paths would never cross again.
I have no idea of what was said, only that

our words echoed off each other, rose up
to create a cloud-shadow
that turned the hills to memory-blue.
For months now I have searched for words

to send you, having forgotten that what
is said is less important than the saying
of it which, when well-intentioned,
forms a cloud-shadow that changes

the landscape, be it the hillside
of bygone days or the future-gorse
out on the island, turned to deepest gold.

Celia de Fréine

Let us go to you

Soles of your feet
burn with longing to walk

time

falls to hopelessness

birds wait
with a song of spring
to weave in sky,
watching
the dancing darkness
and the heat-shy sun

come resist, that walls
be brought down
from foundations
come
let us open up
to the fullest
as we touch yellows
of the poppy
greens of longing

let us go
passing furthest
reaches of villages
as we listen to the
murmured calling
of the rivers

may a hand reach
to hold that which is broken
as the heart moves
through a tunnel
                of impossibility

and let a sparrow
from your palm
fly your words
                to freedom

Ibrahim Altay

The Frame

I sit at my kitchen table in Los Angeles and take account:
There is my childhood house becoming smoke, friends
scattered like storm-blown dandelion seeds, my mother
tongue ripped from my throat.

See the man I used to call husband sinking into the twin
lungs of a beast breathing; like lovers who came and went,
beloveds murdered by their own hands; a homeland
community in jail, shot, hanging from ropes.
That we choose the color
of our loss, like a blue
sash draped across
mourners' black,
that eyes follow blind
towards the cobalt moon,
will bend us over and
down, crooked towards
mud on our graves.

Loss is a language
in the body
we all speak
well, a moan that echoes
between ribs, the downfall
that becomes windfall.

Sholeh Wolpé

A Letter for İlhan

I would send you
the horizon
folded in the crease

of this page. Now
a gesture of sea
that rushes

from it, now
the deep bow
of sky

toward it.
Home
resides in this

line between,
holding its
open gaze.

Nell Regan

As if here I've loved rivers all this time*

I.
Traversed by Tundra swan
courted by White-throated kingfisher,
Gadwall, Lapwing.
Water gleams
 as if stars are trapped in feathers.
And here the sky fills
with varied and vagrant
songs.
        Restless with migration
feathers
            drop
                as if to lessen
 the burden of flight.   Now the earth is
soft
          with down
At rest,
          soft.

II.
Remember as a child how you were held
by a mother / father / uncle as they pointed
to the deer / bird / fox in the distance
saying 'See, see?' And you nodded slowly,
almost a lie, because you wanted to see
whatever wonder their finger aimed toward

that animated their voice,
and you wanted to please
and be more loved for the seeing.

And here you are, first in the forest
this morning, where the river
releases a breath of steam

needles spin in a shaft of light,
one slim ray of new sun points
to an imprint in snow

of the doe's rest, her long hind bones,
curved dome of her back, forelegs folded,
a map of her sleep.

You think, a bird may be caged in my chest
as you kneel to touch the white bed.
How bold she was in her rest
            how miraculous her sleep.

Stella Reed

**Title from a line by Nâzim Hikmet*

The Waiting

After İlhan Çomak

One morning,
your sky will stir and split
into bluebirds—
the breeze an orchestra
of their working wings

You will know the sun again—
how it curls its light
along the earth.
You will know the perfume
and name of each flower

in the soil.
Listen for the air.
Listen for the birds.
They wait for that morning.

Jordan E. Franklin

Studies of an Angel

One
The angel coveted the roof of the house she was assigned to. Her chest pressed against the tarry surface, her arms wrapped protectively around the parapet. Her hands on the viga stubs that protruded below the roof line. The humming sound of family life reverberated her ear. She was smitten. At night, she relaxed her hold a bit. At noon, she escalated the movement of her wings, sending a current of cool air rolling over the home. The house was hers for thirty days, well technically twenty-eight. But she always hung around for an extra day or two to make sure the soul was firmly settled into the newborn body.

Two
The angel coveted the roof of the house. This was it. She had been doing fly-overs for months. Now, as she draped her body over plaster and wood, the fresh smell of amniotic fluid engulfed her. She sensed the mother's milk ducts expanding. Millennia of neonatal guarding had taught her the need for intense focus due to the tenuous hold of the soul in a newborn body. If one slipped out before its time, she could usually trace it to her loss of concentration. The slightest distraction and that soul could squeeze out of any available aperture. Early in her tenure, she hadn't known the free floaters could be so wily. Generally, a soul was accepting of its new position. But every so often, one came along that was in love with the free form adventure and had no interest whatsoever in pulling on the robe of blood and bone again.

Katherine DiBella Seluja

in this dream nothing happens

no *pointless wars of the heart*
though Jupiter and Saturn
have been that close in the early
evening sky the waves
continue their rock and roll there's
memory voices faces
the past on its own arc and the
present arc a rolling curve

nothing in the
dream nothing but a
weaving music sometimes violin
and strings sometimes brass and
voice and those ocean
waves it may be just the
radio (music) it may
just be beach the
dream disappearing in the
dawn and with that the remaining
sleep

Mark Statman

A Heavenly Leaf

İlhan, a single heavenly leaf
dancing in the breeze, on the sky
and under the unfathomable sea.

Even if it is madness to you
he will let himself do so
as a single leaf, beautiful butterfly.

If someone does not like him
Whatever! What is it to him?
It's not the end of the world –
But –
He can fly in the sky.

Mohammad Moheuddin
PEN Bangladesh

The Order of Release

When gates finally
opened there was rejoicing.
It was like a birth.

The miraculous
wore its finest dress and sang
in a pure high voice.

And there were the dreams
stowed away in the wardrobe.
Now they were brought out

like long lost washing.

George Szirtes

The Enclosure Searches for Laws of Enclosure

My invisible ink,
please find a synonym for rivulet.
And what is water made of
besides the inner ear?

Falling, inertia, gravity,
who are you on the stairs of my laughter?
Evolution gave the heart a bone cage,
then grandfather carved a flute.

Oldest radio signal,
did you hear the question about translation?
One, two, three, *bir, iki, üç…*

If a hummingbird is an open window,
who am I saying clerestory?
Deer gather at the pond and I think
this is where they sleep,
the tall grass is bent over.

Mary Cisper

Lit with Lightning

My friend wakes embers in a heap of ash.
She adds wood,
leans in to feed the fire with her breath.

A flaming pyramid grows,
warming us on this cold night in Brooklyn
as we read your words aloud,

> *Buds grumble and thirst for growth.*
> *I look at you, scatter my own ashes.*
> *I go out, add suns to sunlight, walk on seeds.*

 Add suns to sunlight.

> *I praise the embraces of women*
> *that reach right into my cell.*

We praise the sky that inhabits you.
We praise the suns that rise in you.

Around this fire, a friend pours us her potion,
the juice of cherries, laced with lavender and mugwort,
an herb that unspools dreams.

You'll have vivid dreams, she says.

> *I love the bird because we are brothers in hunger…*
> *Let us go blazing to the seas…*

Your dreams will tumble forth in vivid colors.
Drink this down.

What would you want to say to him or give him in a
    poem? I ask.
My friend feeding the fire says, tell him we are listening,
    we hear him.
My friend pouring dreams says, give him a meadow.

A meadow.
Let's visit one in vivid dreams, let's *stand shoulder to shoulder
    with the rain in the uprising scent of soil*

as the drenched earth exhales and trees
shake the storm from their manes.

Shoulder to shoulder, as the sun dries the land
as a dog gives the meadow another pulse,
vanishing and reappearing
from behind the table set for ten,
from behind friends   *silently lit with lightning.*

Silently lit with lightning, we flash like spring clouds
as drummers play, as melons are sprinkled with mint,
    walnuts cracked,
warm bread cut in squares, and cup of that cherry red
    reappears in a friend's hand.

Let us drink dreams inside our dreams.

We praise the sky that inhabits the mind.
We praise poems that are ladders.
We praise words that walk through walls to touch your brow,
    İlhan.

/continued

A light rain falls, a soft whisper of rain,
as if a poet signed the sky.

The walls in him thinned to a silk scrim.
Til they rise to thin down again,
almost transparent.

İlhan, when the sky plants seeds in your eyes,
the ones who listen, see blue.

Haleh Liza Gafori
Lines in italics are by İlhan Sami Çomak

The Pure, Bright Experiment of Rain

I wake in grey dark, place my bare feet
on a threadbare rug that once lay
at the bottom of my grandparents' stairs
and then, when he died, on granny's bathroom floor.
I remember her lifting me out onto it, wrapping a towel
around me. Or maybe I don't, I've made that up –
as you say, in the blazing seas of childhood
we believe in all the stories – but she could have.

I pad out, still in the dark, to make coffee.
I know there's a mouse somewhere
but it's not going to run across my feet
and I wait for water in the one-cup *vriki*
to start that rushing sound it makes
before it boils. Things we do in the secret
life of a house – last night I replaced a bulb
in the ceiling and now, against the black

window, against the pouring night,
these plants on the sill are bright emerald
and I wish I could hand you this coffee.
We could walk up your stairway to the height
of life together, watch a wet blackbird fly down,
waiting for crumbs, we'd talk poetry, laugh
and stare out, safely out, to what you call
the pure, bright experiment of rain.

Ruth Padel

Blue Meta-Pain

My heart becomes
weaker
with the years

of seeing you
grow in a jail
separated from

parents who aged
into white-haired
twins of concern

My heart
was not well
-positioned to see

You, crouched
in jeans and blue shirt
become bent line
colored sapphire
as if you
are the sky

You, crouched
over a bird
with its own cell

Both of you—
a man, a bird—
separated from sky

who would love
men and birds
with as much blue

as vision can project:
*sapphire, cobalt, lapis
lazuli, azure…*

My heart, weakened
by human history,
still imagines—I see

You, standing
looking up
at a sunlit sky

whose infinite expanse
lacks constraints
from any horizon

I see you, standing

Eileen R. Tabios

I Begin to Imagine You Walking Out

After Shipla Gupta 'For, in your tongue, I cannot fit.
2017–2018' where:
    100 microphones are suspended from the ceiling
and reverse-wired to function as speakers. From each,
recitals of a different poet's verse emanate in a
synchronized chorus. Below each microphone the
corresponding verse is spiked on a stand.
Biennale, 2019

we walk between small pillars and light
poems skewered on spikes

each poem a poet in exile
from above their voices a prison

we walk through darkness
the pavement uneven

I want to ask you about prison
but trip on my own privilege

shyness a shield
as I walk into your poems

I have too many rights
walking between small pillars of light

without a *fair trial*
who has any rights?

this *long-gone youth* you have *set aside*
your lifespan a kind of right

we walk among black skewers of light
poets staked to prison beds

your long life
a line in a poem

darkness your only right
while we walk between pillars

your long life a poem
between the moon and the tide

and each stolen year
a stolen human right

Yvonne Blomer
Lines in italics are from interviews and poems
by İlhan Sami Çomak

The Man Who Turned Himself into Poetry

Not true perhaps to say he turned himself.
Rather that poetry seeped and glowed
and leapt and flowed and raged and burned
and ploughed and hoed through him
till he became that which he loved,
a child of poetry true to the child
he carried lovingly in him
through all the years of his imprisonment,
true to his childhood and to that injunction
of Rilke's, proving it and himself,

Until his every utterance became poetry.
Even a photograph of him has this quality:
A man who leaves no trace, who moves through air
with no disturbance, leaving only
a scent of music, the rumour of
the possibility of peace,
the truth contained in hope.

Simon Pettifar
Inspired by Turkish poet Haydar Ergülen's essay
'Poetry of Earth and Sky: The Poetry of İlhan Çomak'

What Life Withholds

Noons, a whole string of them, folded into awaiting,
some colorblind, others blank like bullets. Behind
temples, goldenrod light overwriting the cadence
of the hours. Frost-faced, this November unwings
its blues and eyes dream of tiptoed trees, bleeding
green, lush tongues swaying their tilt. Once upon
another autumn, you held baby dawns in your mouth,
and restlessness filled your pockets. Now, time coils
around your ankles like ancient fumes, yet ink oozes
from your lips for others to sip you softly, like balm.
Cold flowers of the mind blooming in raw discipline.

Clara Burghelea

Word of Mouth

What remains of us will be our voices, not locked in towering
silence or staunched or lopped by the inhospitable, dry as
medical text. Cut loose, our vowels winging through hushed *h's*,
our heads will roll and we'll forget what dungeons. We'll be
acrobats on moonshine tangled in loops of saliva, tears will
twinkle in our I's. We'll muddle our speech through slippery
tunnels, worming out words to suck indignity from injury. Like
armagnac, the way it warms to good old sorrow, a mithridatic
bee brew, a salve for a poor exile's throat to swallow. Take
note, take heart! As a walnut cracks another walnut, in the
palms of our distress, pressed, by sweet and sound intention,
broken open.

Cally Conan-Davies

Two Points Determine a Line

In the silence between wakefulness and sleep, I form these
words of friendship, ink into pixels into ink. In the silence,
the wall has something to say by its own silence, and the earth
that rises and dips through ocean, continent to continent. A
feeling that travels through any medium. Earthquake, tsunami.
The flutter of leaves fastened still to the bough, persevering
into a fullness of fiery reds tipped gold.

In the silence of the high desert, dark shapes cluster in the reach
of pines nestled in the fold of a mountain road rising from a
narrow in the canyon floor. Heavy rustle of wings, a dark shape
in flux. Once in the silence of dawn I saw outspread wings
collecting the warmth of sunlight grazing the treetops.
A single bird.

In the silence, the surprise of snow, deer under the uplift of an
old maple. They step curious like words, startling into the air in
quick leaps. Four, ten bodies bounding in the night, small and
large, the rush, the rustle. *Life does not lie*, you write.

Jane Lin

Juniper

The scent of the rain
And juniper
Like the river & the sounds
Of the wind, waves
Repeating
Paddles in the meadow
The clouds afloat
I taste the orange
& wonder
If I could ever recover
From this swollen heart
This red
What I don't understand
These lines, these walls
Limits, resounding
notes of juniper
The woody green
Of fresh linen, the grey shadow
In the sun I am warm
I don't know how long I am to wait
I feel as though
I am fading
Pale flowers on the wallpaper in the sun
I want to rise
But I don't know
How far, how long

Meg Kaizu

Sometimes He Dreams

Sometimes he dreams of his mother's pomegranate smile,
of himself as a wide-eyed boy, listening to folk tales,
watching shadows flicker on the wall behind the stove.

He remembers how they all used to sit in the warm glow,
hugging their knees, while the wind howled outside.

They felt safe then, hearing those tales of heroes
fighting monsters, killing villains.

In his prison cell, he tries to stay asleep.
He wants to put his arms round that boy,
stop him walking into the future.

Kelly Davis
Inspired by İlhan Sami Çomak's letter,
January 2020

Awaken Spirit and Eat

The grass is hungry for love's touch.
Yesterday Mother Earth gave her tears
to caress the blades in the meadow.

I saw you there on bended knees
stroking blades of grass
to soothe your heavy heart.

I bend my knees to honor your
words as they rise from the flames
of your heartfelt garden.

You are not alone in your struggle
to give your soul freedom.
Spirit lines the path for you.

The trail glows with love's candlelight.
Nothing can destroy the light
that streams from the heavenly planes.

Breathe in, breathe out
as the love of Spirit
nourishes your soul.

Teresa E. Gallion

For İlhan Çomak

When I think of you,
I remember my own incarceration,
which was only for a short time,
and which I could have avoided
by turning in a friend,
but instead I went in with him.

Inside the jail,
I was lied to, made false promises to,
stripped of my belongings,
housed with cockroaches,
fed unfamiliar food in a soft container,
and generally ignored.

And my time there was only for a nanosecond
compared with many years.
And my discomfort was only a nano-part
of what you have endured.
But I can look back on it,
and I hope that someday—soon—you can, too.

I hope that your spirits will be lifted
in the midst of what seems unliftable,
and you will find courage
in the midst of the un-encourageable.
And I hope these words find their way to you
like rays of pale light or sounds of faint music
through some unstoppable space
in the wall that separates us.

Thaddeus Rutowski

Timeless Waters

Thinking about time: wondering
how much time is left: whether
it's time to start detaching   time
to clear: ah yes, clear
                              clear water

To drink a glass of clear water
float on a green and blue ocean:
the feel of water   the movement
of water
                against my skin

Is this what death will be like:
return to that warm amniotic
fluid   return to the ocean:
to those timeless
     waters of life.

Ruth Fainlight

The Goat's Wounded Eye

I'm imprisoned in my people's
voice that they failed to let out.
I try giving weight to the soundless
cry, but like the star in my mind
that holds my eye, I fail. I never
get beyond the horizon's dreary
line, moon's signature supposed
to release me from a dawn that never
arrives. My room is dark, still.
I open the window for starlight,
hearing bleats of pain, realizing
I was the boy that cried.

Jonel Abellanosa

Untitled

Here I am in fragmented versions of sun,
the scale of small fruits.
When someone bends to tell the infinite timorous
middle of goodbye, I hear it

loose as a hymn. I don't mind all the hauntings:
each displacement of air, the clocks
yawning in a practice to tire.
Down the road, signs and wounds.

I climb the hill for some gritty tea.
To watch a listing crowd of robins vector
for water in the dish we put out.
Any need can loop into prayer.

Lauren Camp

For İlhan Sami Çomak

Released and reinvented to no state,
she clambered up on her girlfriend's shoulders
to hold a torch, pointing at the prancing troubadour
and singing praise to the wilderness.

It was in nature her truth was told
but the animals had been herded for meat confusion,
the psychosis in the transference of their bodies
to the imperialism of man had clouded the organic soul.

She had plans to start a band to keep the peace,
strange but true and the singer in his mind,
in bird song mystic, thought the line, I love you.

Thurston Moore

The Captive's Song

For İlhan Çomak on 'Day of the Imprisoned Writer'

To be banished, boots thrust in
belly and back, shoulders dislocated—
simply to keep you down.

Tear out your tongue.
Circle cold concrete,
cracked paint, mould on a wall—

Impoverished. Imprisoned—
and yet, Poet, in your solitary cave,
diligently refining, *redefining* resilience;

a musculature of words,
the activist's inner ear—
non-violent resistance.

I want to send you words of comfort, solidarity—
affirm I oppose the terrible manner in which you are oppressed.

But even as I lift my pen, your marvellous,
life-affirming poems arrive on my threshold;
fertile images of sky and sun from your sunless, skyless cell—

humbling emissaries turning the tables;

Wake up, I hear you urge, gently. *Unlock your jaded
    windows and doors.
Open yourself to the extraordinary freedoms of your
    ordinary day.*

Sophia Wilson

Love Charm

The ruby throated hummingbird drinking
from the tiny red trumpet blossoms
of the willowy licorice mint, is oblivious of me,
standing close, with my watering can.
I straighten a finger and touch the bird's
warm, full center. A drop of nectar, like sorrow
from an eye, falls from its beak. Its mouth—
overflowing with the syrup of the flower—
can hold no more. And still it drinks and drinks.
In animal medicine, hummingbird conjures affection;
its feathers are used to make love charms,
and just like desire, a hummingbird
can fly in any direction.

Elizabeth Jacobson

Licorice *mint*:
https://en.wikipedia.org/wiki/Agastache rupestris

In the Palm of My Hand, Rivers

Because the fields of my childhood
vanished, I carry smoke in my hair.
I bed dank dirt in my hands.

My father shook his wars, sank
the hum of their dangers in mud.
The deeper he dug, the more
it smelled like bread. Mothers
placed seeds in the graves
of those guns. I have not
forgotten the rivers that flowed
underground. How the cottonwood
roots sipped, made ships for my brothers and me.

We sailed to places where trees
were called *palm*. Where night's catharsis
couldn't break us. If days were fruit, those
days were plums, succulent in their viscid
light and endless sources of juice. When Fall
turned leaves to breezing husks, we blanketed
in mulch, with bulbs making food of the ground.

Tina Carlson

Wild Grapes

What hand brings light into your tendrils?
What light paints such red and green along your meridians?
What force fills up your veins with sap of passion, will to live?
What heart gives you the courage to live, under any
    condition or hostility?
What wind, what poetry, what key, opens the secret door
    to your zest for life?

Wang Ping

Inventing the Land

Now this is what you shall do—

Take the land each way
you dream a lover   earth skin
seamless against her found beauty

No map for this country called flame
Sky   the supple throat of fire   tasting
amethyst   bittersweet   cerulean

Ride some road to that place with no name
past ripe-veined streams pierced by twilight
heat blood in rock soil pulsing and blazed

Andrea Watson

Who'd Have Thought

From 'Thirteen Angels'

the debris of those unregarded lives,
the words choked in their throats,
their fluent silences bricked in by noise,

could constitute an angel?
But look at the stress lines spreading
through the concrete at your feet,

cracks feathering, flexing, dust-flakes
crumbling, as it rises; the crackling
sound as it fills out its wings.

The first downbeat is clumsy;
it gathers its mass, bundled armfuls of flight,
and flings it. The horizons shudder

like the tacky backdrop we half knew
they were. It clears its throat
like white noise, like a waterfall, like wind.

Philip Gross

The Light I Hold

The prison key opens wide
Fields where my wounds are
Poppies of love and hope.

Walls are rivers,
Breath is wind
Words are trees.

But the blood you spill is
Choking your sons
Your fists are empty
Your seeds are weeds.

The light I hold will never fade.

Luca Paci

each star so

solitary
seized within
light as cells are

by what holds form
firm through
time

at last
the prisoner
sees the bars he is

made from as only that
which divides his
prisons

through
steely rungs in
that sidewise climb

to what seems an end
where difference
flares

shone
through those
spaces thinking makes

as absent without it as
unfathered sons
& how

to pass
that on except
through far & single g-

hosts hotly aware but
dimly in others'
pull as

they burn
dark through
to light my dust

made before
i knew it
dust

Mario Petrucci

Shadow World

Ghazal

Say the end of the world fell on a Saturday—
     would it then remain that Saturday forever?

Or what if one grey morning you woke up to find
     the world was not the same, but had changed forever?

That suddenly your life, the world you knew so well,
     was not the life you thought would be yours forever?

Or that those dear to you, both close and far away,
     were part of your world no longer, lost forever?

Would you retreat into the world of your small room,
     your even smaller bed, and lie down forever?

Or would you curse your fate, and rail against your god,
     then pray for your world to be restored forever?

Maybe you'd fling your fist, defy the world's new face,
     resolve to conquer fate if it took forever?

Or what if, abruptly, an endless night-time fell,
     not on the world but on your spirit, forever?

Would you yearn for a day your shadow world might burst
        free of its nightmare, pledging a fresh forever?

Or would you look around and for the first time see
        that though the world had altered, *now* was forever?

That the whole world was now, and now was what *you* were,
        and it was always now, and would be forever?

For as I write these lines it's Saturday no more
        and the world keeps turning—now, if not forever

Alex Skovron

Window

Sometimes a city is shown its own
reflection in the sky, as if to insist
on another world, which is not really there
though its streets are positioned correctly.

The same is true when you reach the end
of an avenue and turn to watch the traffic
dissolve into a silver stream in the distance
you have come from. Or when you climb a hill

to see the city far below at daybreak
laid out like a map – as if all its pieces
could be counted and measured, and you could point
to your own life unfolding among them.

Ian Seed

Unseen

Is it true, as they say,
most people are never seen,
but walk through their lives like the dead?

I do not know, but I know
a man behind walls can be seen
because words are masters of escape.

They are free like the crow,
misread friend of the dark who draws
some of that darkness into the day,

refusing the beautiful song.
Persisting, intelligent, he will not
countenance illusions or kowtow to idiots.

That is why, more than the spangled parrot,
he is honored by those who see him.

David Mason

Author and Translator Biographies

Jonel Abellanosa lives in Cebu City, in the Philippines. Nominated for the Pushcart, Dwarf Stars and Best of the Net awards. His poetry collections include *Songs from My Mind's Tree* and *Multiverse* (Clare Songbirds Publishing House, New York), *50 Acrostic Poems*, (Cyberwit, India), *In the Donald's Time* (Poetic Justice Books and Art, Florida), *Instrumentals* (Lemures Press), and *Pan's Saxophone* (Weasel Press, Texas).

Ibrahim Altay is a Cypriot poet and translator whose poems and translations have been published in various literary magazines. His first book *Gitme Biçimleri - Ways of Leaving* was published in 2024.

Michael Geoffrey Baron was born in London. He is co-founder of the National Autistic Society for which he received an MBE. He initiated the annual Words by the Water literary festival in Keswick and has edited/co-edited several anthologies. His collections include *More than a Man in a Boat (*self-published, 2005) and *The Gingko Tree (*Palewell Press, 2023).

Yvonne Blomer is an award-winning poet and nonfiction writer. She is the author of six books of poems and has edited five anthologies. Yvonne holds an MA with Distinction from the University of East Anglia and is the past poet laureate of Victoria, BC. She lives on the territories of the Lək̓ʷəŋən (Lekwungen) speaking people.

Clara Burghelea has two published poetry collections: *The Flavor of the Other* (Dos Madres Press, 2020) and *Praise the Unburied* (Chaffinch Press, 2021). Her poems and translations have been published in *Goalf Coast, Delos, The Los Angeles Review,* and elsewhere. She is the Review Editor of *Ezra, An Online Journal of Translation* and a third-year PhD student in Literature at the University of Texas in Dallas.

Lauren Camp serves as New Mexico Poet Laureate. She is the author of eight books of poetry, most recently *In Old Sky* (Grand Canyon Conservancy, 2024). A former Astronomer-in-Residence at Grand Canyon National Park, Camp has been a finalist for the Arab American

Book Award, New Mexico-Arizona Book Award, and Adrienne Rich Award.

Tina Carlson is a New Mexico poet and mental health provider. She has published three full-length collections of poetry: *Ground, Wind, This Body, We Are Meant to Carry Water* (in collaboration with two other NM poets), and *A Guide to Tongue Tie Surgery*. Her chapbook *Obsidian* was published in 2024. She is an editor of the online journal *Unbroken.*

John Casquarelli is the author of *On Equilibrium of Song* (Overpass Books, 2011), *Lavender* (Authorspress, 2014), and *Late Evening in a Paladares* (Alien Buddha Press, 2023). He is a Lecturer at Koç Üniversitesi in Istanbul. John received his MFA in Creative Writing at Long Island University-Brooklyn, studying under Lewis Warsh, John High, and Anne Waldman. His poems have appeared in numerous journals and anthologies.

Mary Cisper is a poet living in northern New Mexico. Her award-winning poetry collection, *Dark Tussock Moth*, was published by Trio House. She publishes books at Thixotropic Press in cooperation with C. Pirloul

Cally Conan-Davies was born in Hobart, Tasmania in 1960. Since completing her post-graduate studies in English and Psychology at Monash University, Melbourne, she has taught at secondary and post-secondary levels, worked as a bibliotherapist and freelance writer. Cally founded Lit For Life Centre for Creative Reading and her poetry has appeared in many journals.

Kelly Davis is a freelance editor and poet, living in West Cumbria. She collaborated with Kerry Darbishire on *Glory Days* (Grey Hen Press, 2021) and her first solo collection *The Lost Art of Ironing* (Hedgehog Poetry Press) was published in 2024.

Isobel Dixon won the Sanlam and Olive Schreiner prizes for her debut poetry collection *Weather Eye* (Carapace, 2001). Her further collections, *A Fold in the Map* and *The Tempest Prognosticator,* originally published by Salt, were both republished by Nine Arches in

2018. Nine Arches published her latest collection, *A Whistling of Birds* (with 12 illustrations by Douglas Robertson), in 2023.

Gabriel Don undertook her MFA in creative writing (Fiction and Non-Fiction) at The New School, where she worked as the Reading Series and Chapbook Competition Coordinator. Her poetry collection, *Living Without Skin*, was released with A Gathering of The Tribes, Fly By Night Press and featured at the Whitney Biennial in 2022. Born in Australia, raised in Singapore and Dubai, Don now lives in New York.

Theo Dorgan is a poet, non-fiction writer, novelist, editor, documentary screenwriter, essayist, librettist and translator from Ireland.

Menna Elfyn is an award-winning poet and playwright from Wales who writes in Welsh but whose work has been translated into over twenty languages. She has published sixteen collections of poetry, children's novels, libretti for UK and US composers as well as plays for television and radio.

Ruth Fainlight is an American-born poet, short story writer, translator and librettist based in the United Kingdom, and a Fellow of the Royal Society of Literature. Her published work includes 16 poetry collections.

Blas Falconer is the author of *Rara Avis* (Four Way Books 2024); *Forgive the Body This Failure* (Four Way Books, 2018); *The Foundling Wheel* (Four Way Books, 2012); *A Question of Gravity and Light* (University of Arizona Press, 2007); and *The Perfect Hour* (Pleasure Boat Studio: A Literary Press, 2006). He teaches in the MFA program at San Diego State University.

Jordan E. Franklin is a Black poet from New York, whose work has appeared widely in journals. She won the 2017 James Hearst Poetry Prize, and was a finalist in both the 2019 Nightjar Poetry Contest and the 2019 Furious Flower Poetry Prize. Her debut poetry collection, *when the signals come home* won the 2020 Gatewood Prize.

Celia de Fréine is a poet, playwright and screenwriter who writes in Irish and English.

Haleh Liza Gafori is a New York City-born translator, performance artist, writer, and educator of Persian descent. A 2024 MacDowell fellow, she has translated the poetry of the Persian mystic and sage Rumi. Her book of translations entitled *Gold: Poems by Rumi*, was published by New York Review Books in 2022. She is currently working on the second volume.

Teresa E. Gallion is a poet who lives in the Southwestern United States of America. She has published five books of poetry: *Walking Sacred Ground, Contemplation in the High Desert, Chasing Light*, a 2013 book award finalist, *Scent of Love*, a 2021 book award finalist and her most recent book is *Come Egypt*. Her work has appeared in numerous journals and anthologies.

Philip Gross has published 30 collections in 40 years, including *The Shores of Vaikus*, a re-inhabiting of Estonia, his refugee father's birthplace (2024). He won the T.S. Eliot Prize in 2010.

Øivind Hånes is a Norwegian teacher, writer, editor, record producer, active musician, composer and author. His books have been translated into German, Spanish, Dutch, Russian and Lithuanian.

Lee Herrick is the California Poet Laureate. He is the author of four books of poems. Lee was born in Daejeon, Korea, and adopted as an infant. He lives with his family in Fresno, California. He teaches at Fresno City College and in the low-residency MFA program at University of Nevada Reno at Lake Tahoe. He is the 10th California Poet Laureate, and the first Asian American to serve in the role.

Elizabeth Jacobson was the fifth Poet Laureate of Santa Fe, New Mexico, and an Academy of American Poets 2020 Laureate Fellow.

Megumi Kaizu is an artist, writer, and translator. She has exhibited her artwork internationally, and published her poetry, fiction, essays, reviews, and translation in anthologies and journals such as *Words Without Borders* and *Brooklyn Rails*.

Jane Lin is the author of *Day of Clean Brightness* (3: A Taos Press, 2017). She is a poet and a software engineer for an environmental consulting company. Jane was born and raised on Long Island, NY, and lives in Northern New Mexico where she taught creative writing for many years at UNM-Los Alamos.

Aasne Linnestå (1963) is a Norwegian poet, novelist and librettist, having published five collections of poetry and eight novels, and has also written three librettos for composer and musician Maja S.K. Ratkje.

John Macker, poet, playwright and essayist, has lived in Northern New Mexico for 28 years. His most recent books are *Belated Mornings, Atlas of Wolves, The Blues Drink Your Dreams Away: Selected Poems1983–2018, El Rialto* (a memoir), and *Desert Threnody*, essays and short fiction.

David Mason is a teacher, poet and editor, born in the USA. His poetry collections include *The Buried Houses* (1991); *The Country I Remember* (1996); *Arrivals* (2004); and the verse novel *Ludlow* (2007), awarded the Colorado Book Award for Poetry and named best book of poetry in 2007 by the *Contemporary Poetry Review.*

Liz McManus is a novelist and poet and member of Irish PEN. She is former Deputy Leader of the Labour Party and was a columnist with the *Sunday Tribune*. Winner of the Hennessy Short Story Award and many other literary prizes.

Mohammad Moheuddin is a fiction writer and editor of *Golpokar*, the only monthly fiction magazine in Bangla. He is the secretary-general of PEN Bangladesh. He has published ten novels and two short story books.

Thurston Moore is an American musician and writer, born 1958, living and working in London, married, two dogs, a couple of guitars, digging 66. He founded the New York City music group Sonic Youth. His most recent release is *Spirit Counsel*. He teaches writing at the Jack Kerouac School of Disembodied Poetics.

Steinar Opstad is a Norwegian poet. He made his literary debut in 1996 with the poetry collection *Tavler og bud*, which earned him Tarjei Vesaas' debutantpris. He was awarded the Aschehoug Prize in 2003 and the Herman Wildenvey Poetry Award in 2015.

Alice Oswald studied Classics at Oxford and then trained as a gardener. Her first book of poems was *The Thing in the Gap-Stone Stile*, which won the Forward Prize in 1996. She won the T.S. Eliot Prize for her long poem *Dart*. In 2009 she won a Cholmondeley award for her contribution to poetry. She was the Oxford Professor of Poetry between 2019 and 2023.

Luca Paci works as a lecturer, poet, editor and translator between English and Italian. His translations include works by Elio Pagliarani and Menna Elfyn, and he edited *Tempo: Excursions in 21st-Century Italian Poetry.*

Ruth Padel is an award-winning British poet, novelist and non-fiction writer, with close links to Greece, India, classical music, nature, science and wildlife conservation.

Torgeir Rebolledo Pedersen is a Norwegian architect, poet, playwright and author of children's books. He made his literary debut in 1983 with the poetry collection *Tidr* and has since published several collections. He was awarded the Dobloug Prize in 2013.

Mario Petrucci is a British-Italian poet, literary translator, educator and broadcaster. He was born in London and trained as a physicist at the University of Cambridge, later completing a PhD in vacuum crystal growth at University College London. Among his publications is *Tales from the Bridge*. Shortlisted for the 2012 Ted Hughes award, it was the world's largest 3D poetry soundscape and a centerpiece of the London Cultural Olympiad.

Simon Pettifar lives in a small town straddling the Welsh-English border. He writes poems, organises occasional readings with musicians, translates Czech poet Jan Skácel and notices that he has an instinctive aversion to all walls and fences. He is writing a screenplay based on the life of American writer Nathanael West.

Wang Ping is a poet, writer, photographer, performance and multimedia artist. Her award-winning books include four collections of poetry, *The Magic Whip, Of Flesh & Spirit, Ten Thousand Waves*, and *My Name Is Immigrant*; the novel *Foreign Devil*; two collections of fiction stories entitled *American Visa* and *The Last Communist Virgin*;

a book of Chinese folklore, *The Dragon Emperor*; and a book of creative nonfiction, *Life of Miracles along the Yangtze and Mississippi*.

Leeanne Quinn is an Irish poet. She holds a PhD in American Literature from Trinity College Dublin. Her first collection of poetry, *Before You*, was published by Dedalus Press in 2012. Her second collection, *Some Lives*, was published in 2020. She lives in Vienna, Austria.

Stella Reed (she/her) is the co-author of the AZ-NM Book Award-winning *We Are Meant to Carry Water,* 2019, from 3: A Taos Press. She is the winner of the Jacar Press Chapbook Prize for *Myth from the field where the fox runs with its tail on fire* and the Tusculum Review chapbook contest for *Origami.* You can find her work in various journals and anthologies throughout the US, in Ireland, and Australia.

Nell Regan is a poet and non-fiction writer and recent recipient of the Patrick and Katherine Kavanagh Fellowship. She is an educator and literary programmer based in Dublin and her latest book is *A Gap in the Clouds: A New Translation of Ogura Hyakunin Isshu,* translated with James Hadley (Dedalus, 2021)

Thaddeus Rutkowski is the author of eight books of prose and poetry, most recently *Safe Colors*, a novel in short fictions. His novel *Haywire* won the members' choice award from the Asian American Writers' Workshop. He teaches at Medgar Evers College, Columbia University, and a YMCA, and received a fiction writing fellowship from the New York Foundation for the Arts.

Ian Seed is an award-winning poet, prose poet, translator, short-story writer, essayist and editor. His collection of prose poetry, *New York Hotel* (Shearsman, 2018) was featured on BBC Radio Merseyside and was a *TLS* Book of the Year, while *Identity Papers* (Shearsman, 2016) and *Makers of Empty Dreams* (Shearsman, 2014) were showcased on BBC Radio Three's *The Verb*.

Katherine DiBella Seluja is a poet and micro fiction writer and the author of *Point of Entry* (UNM Press, 2023), *Gather the Night* (UNM Press, 2018), and co-author of the award-winning collection, *We Are Meant to Carry Water* (3: A Taos Press, 2019). Her poem, 'November

Fruit', is part of the Taos Poetry in Nature Project and is on permanent display at the Helene Wurlitzer Foundation in Taos, New Mexico.

Alex Skovron is an editor and writer, the author of seven collections of poetry, a prose novella and a book of short stories. His collections include *Letters from the Periphery* (2021); *Towards the Equator* (2014), shortlisted in the Prime Minister's Literary Awards; *The Attic*, a selection of his poetry translated into French (2013); and a volume of Chinese translations, *Water Music* (2017).

Mark Statman is a writer, translator, and poet. He is emeritus Professor of Literary Studies at Eugene Lang College, the New School for Liberal Arts in New York City, where he taught from 1985 to 2016. He has published 13 books, eight of poetry, three of translation, and two on pedagogy and poetry.

Caroline Stockford is a Welsh poet, writer and translator of Turkish literature and poetry. Her essays, short stories and translations have been published in Europe, North America and Africa. She works as Turkey Adviser for PEN Norway.

George Szirtes's *Reel* (2004) won the T.S. Eliot Prize for which he has been twice shortlisted since. He won the Booker Prize for translation in 2015.

Eileen R. Tabios has released books of poetry, fiction, art, essays, and experimental writings from publishers around the world. Her body of work includes a first poetry book, *Beyond Life Sentences*, which received the Philippines' National Book Award for Poetry, and invention of the hay(na)ku, a 21st century diasporic poetic form.

Erkut Tokman is a Turkish poet, translator, visual/performance artist, and a member of the Poetry Society and Exiled Writers Ink as well as both Turkish and Italian PEN. He is the author of seven verse collections and has recent poems in *New Humanist* and *Poetry Buenos Aires*. He won the Italian Ministry of Culture Translation and Quasimodo Jaci Poetry awards.

Anne Waldman is an American poet. Waldman has written more than 60 books. Since the 1960s, she has been an active member of the

Outriders Poetry Project experimental poetry community as a writer, performer, collaborator, professor, editor, scholar, and cultural/political activist. She has also been connected to the Beat Generation poets.

Andrea Watson is the founding publisher of 3: A Taos Press. Her poetry has appeared in *The Feminist Journal of Studies in Religion,* and *The Dublin Quarterly,* among others. She is co-editor of the poetry anthologies, *Collecting Life: Poets on Objects Known and Imagined* and *Malala: Poems for Malala Yousafzai.* Andrea has designed and curated 18 *ekphrasis* events across the United States.

Sophia Wilson lives in Aotearoa (New Zealand). An arts graduate and former mental health worker, she is the recipient of several poetry awards including for her collection *Sea Skins* (Flying Island Books, 2023).

Sholeh Wolpé is an Iranian-American poet, playwright, and librettist. Her most recent work includes *Abacus of Loss: A Memoir in Verse* (University of Arkansas Press), *Abaco de Perdida* (Visor Libros, 2025), and *The Invisible Sun – Attar* (Harper Collins, 2025). She is the poetry editor at *The Markaz Review* and a Writer-In-Residence at the University of California, Irvine.

Jeffrey Cyphers Wright received his MFA after studying with Allen Ginsberg. A New Romantic poet, he is also a publisher, art and literary critic, eco-activist, impresario, filmmaker, and artist. His 20 books of verse include *Blue Lyre, Party Everywhere,* and *Doppelängster, Self Portraits in a Funhouse Mirror* (MadHat Press). Wright publishes *Live Mag!* His films and puppet shows are on YouTube.

Palewell Press

Palewell Press is an independent publisher handling poetry, fiction and non-fiction with a focus on books that foster Justice, Equality and Sustainability. The Editor can be reached on
enquiries@palewellpress.co.uk

www.ingramcontent.com/pod-product-compliance
Lightning Source LLC
Chambersburg PA
CBHW070444170726
48291CB00005B/1593